A New True Book

TIME

D0131122

By Feenie Ziner and Elizabeth Thompson

TABLE OF CONTENTS

 CHILDRENS PRESS, CHICAGO

Sunset

DAY AND NIGHT

How do you know what time it is?

You can tell something about time by looking at the sun.

It is morning at sunrise.

It is noon when the sun is highest in the sky.

It is evening when the sun sets.

At night the moon shines on Earth. At the same time the sun is shining on the other side of the Earth.

When the sun shines on the other side of our planet Earth, it is night for us.

But you cannot count hours just by looking at the sun.

SHADOW STICKS

A shadow stick can help us count the hours.

A shadow stick points straight up. The stones around the stick mark the hours.

A shadow stick is like a clock.

As the Earth turns, the
sun makes the shadow of
the stick fall on the stones.

8

The shadow moves from one stone to the next in one hour.

Can you tell time on a cloudy day with a shadow stick?

No.

Can you tell time at night with a shadow stick?

No.

Two examples of American sundials

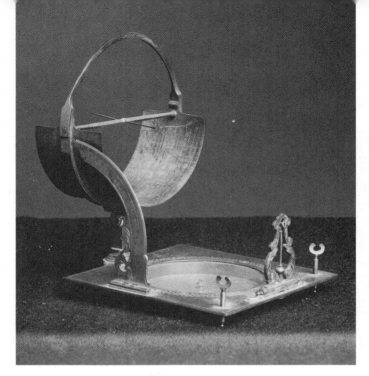

Although this sundial has a different shape, it works just like the sundials shown on page 10.

SUNDIALS

A sundial is like a shadow stick. It can only tell time when the sun is shining.

CANDLE CLOCKS

There is a way to tell time that works both night and day.

It works when it is sunny or cloudy.

It is a candle clock.

A candle clock is painted with bands of color. It takes an hour for each band to burn.

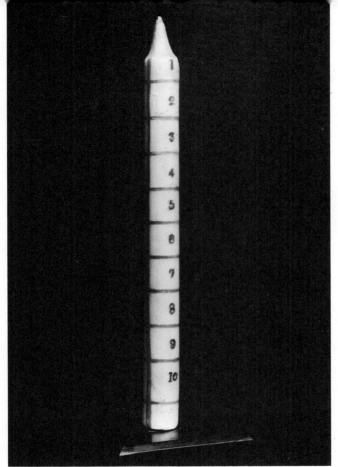

Model of a
King Alfred
candle clock

If you light a candle clock at 8 o'clock and burn 2 bands what time will it be?

Ten o'clock.

14 Example of a time rope, part of the
Smithsonian Institution's collection

ROPE CLOCKS

People can count hours by burning ropes. They tie knots in the rope to mark the hours.

People in Korea once used rope clocks.

It takes one hour for the rope to burn from one knot to the next.

Candle clocks and rope clocks do not need the sun.

Can the candle clock or the rope clock be used over again?

No.

Ancient Egyptian water clock made about 2200 years ago

WATER CLOCKS

Water clocks were used long, long ago.

The first water clock measured the water leaking out of a big pot.

Different water lines were marked on the pot— one for each hour. People could tell time by looking at the line and the water left in the pot.

Water clocks did not need the sun. They could work at night. They could be used over and over again.

HOURGLASS

Another way of telling time is with an hourglass. It has an unusual shape.

Sand falls from the top to the bottom.

This takes one hour.

Then the glass is turned upside down.

An hourglass and a water clock can be used again and again.

HOW TO TELL TIME

Do you know how to tell time?

Or do you ask someone else, "What time is it?"

The short hand points to 3. It is 3 o'clock.

People look at the clock
to find out what time it is.
How does the clock tell
them the time?
The short hand points to
the hours.

It takes an hour for the short hand to move from one number to the next.

There are 24 hours in a day. A day lasts from midnight to midnight. This is how much time it takes the Earth to turn around once.

The Earth turns once every 24 hours.

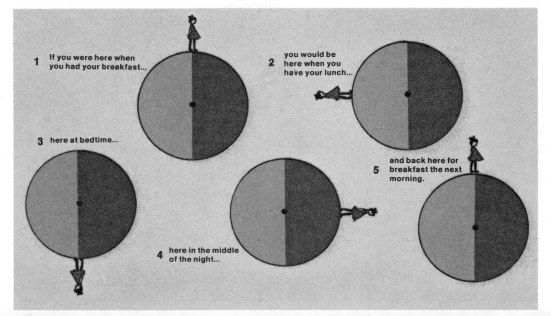

1 If you were here when you had your breakfast...

2 you would be here when you have your lunch...

3 here at bedtime...

4 here in the middle of the night...

5 and back here for breakfast the next morning.

The long hand points to
the minutes. There are 60
minutes in an hour.

The long hand goes all around the clock once every hour. It tells how many minutes after the hour it is.

It takes 5 minutes for the long hand to move from one number to the next.

Most clocks count minutes by fives.

Some clocks count seconds, too. There are 60 seconds in a minute.

Above: Clock using Arabic numerals
Left: Clock using Roman numerals

Most clocks have numbers from 1 to 12. But some clocks have special numbers called Roman numerals.

Can you tell time on this kind of clock?

The chart tells you what the Roman numerals mean. Now can you tell what time it is? If you said 6 o'clock, you are correct.

Roman numeral		Arabic numeral
I	equals	1
II	=	2
III	=	3
IV	=	4
V	=	5
VI	=	6
VII	=	7
VIII	=	8
IX	=	9
X	=	10
XI	=	11
XII	=	12

You know that when the clock reads 12 o'clock during the day it is noontime. Noon is the middle of the day. Most people eat around noontime.

At night when the short hand points to 12 it is midnight. This is the middle of the night. Most people are asleep at midnight.

On most clocks, the short hand goes around two times in 24 hours.

A 24-hour clock on display at the Museum of Science and Industry in Chicago, Illinois

24-HOUR CLOCKS

Some clocks are 24-hour clocks. Each hour of the day has its own number.

On this clock at noon the hour hand would point to 12. When the hour hand points to 00 it would be midnight. Midnight is hour number 24.

Above: 12-hour clock
Right: 24-hour clock

Look at these two clocks. One is a 12-hour clock. The other is a 24-hour clock.

The 12 hour clock reads 2 o'clock and the sun is shining. At 2 o'clock what number would the hour hand point to on the 24-hour clock? Remember each hour has its own number.

Did you say 14? If you were telling time on a 24-hour clock, the hour hand would be pointing to 14.

The army uses the 24-hour clock. With this clock there is no mistake about night and day because each hour has its own number.

Early digital clock
made by Gillett and
Craydon about 1880

DIGITAL CLOCKS

Today we have clocks
that do not have hands.
They are called digital
clocks. Do you know how
to tell time on this kind of
clock?

Look at this clock. The first number shown tells you the hour.

It is 3 o'clock.

The number after the colon tells you the minutes. It is 12 minutes after the hour.

Plato digital clock made by E.L. Fitch, New York, in 1902. This was one of the four basic models made by the Ansonia Clock Company.

A modern digital clock

Can you tell what time it
is on the two clocks
shown on page 38?

The top clock tells you it
is 4 o'clock. On the other
clock the time is 2:56. It
is 56 minutes after 2 o'clock.
In four more minutes
it will be 3 o'clock.
Remember there are 60
minutes in an hour.

Sometimes it is hard to tell the hour hand from the minute hand.
But if you look closely you can see a difference. This clock
tells you it's 21 minutes after twelve.

THINGS TO REMEMBER

The short hand points to the hours.

It takes one hour for the short hand to move from one number to the next.

There are 24 hours in a day.

The long hand points to the minutes in an hour. There are 5 minutes between each number. The long hand tells how many minutes after the hour it is.

Clocks are made
in all sizes and
shapes.

Big Ben is a famous clock in London, England.

The long hand moves all around the clock while the short hand is going from one number to the next.

There are 60 seconds in one minute.

Some clocks are 24-hour clocks. Each hour has its own number.

WORDS YOU SHOULD KNOW

Arabic numerals(AIR • ih • bik NOOM • er • ilz) — The numbers 1, 2, 3, 4, 5, 6, 7, 8, 9, and 0

candle clock(KAN • dil CLAHK) — a candle painted with bands of color that take one hour each to burn

digital clock(DIJ • ih • til CLAHK) — a clock that tells time in number units

hour(OUR) — a unit of time that is equal to sixty minutes

hourglass(OUR • glass) — an instrument used to measure time

minute(MIN • it) — a unit of time equal to sixty seconds

noon — middle of the day; twelve o'clock in the daytime

queer(KWEER) — unusual; odd; strange

Roman numerals(ROH • min NOOM • er • ilz) — letters used by ancient Romans to stand for numbers. For example I=1, V=5, X=10, L=50, C=100, D=500 M=1000

shadow stick(SHAD • oh STIK) — an instrument used to measure time by the sun

sundial(SUN • dyle) — an instrument used to tell time by the sun

The Children's Reading Institute offers several card learning programs for development of reading and math skills. For information write to Children's Reading Institute, Drawer 709, Higganum, CT 06441.